Emotions of Everything

Kassie Corica

BookLeaf
Publishing

Presentation by *BookLeaf Publishing*

Web: www.bookleafpub.com

E-mail: info@bookleafpub.com

ISBN: 9789357440110

First edition 2023

To my son Gavin

Breathe

Inhale
Air dense with hope fills the hollow cavity
within
What was once a heaviness begins to dissipate
Exhale
Light slowly creeps in, a foreign presence
A stranger inside lulling you to join
Inhale
The thick void now infused with luster
A gleam that's unfamiliar you contemplate
squander
Exhale
Internal smog replaced with glistening
A yearning for life now resides

Ecstacy

You came back at the perfect time
A moment when our hearts could realign
Now healed from a past of sorrow
You bring light into a forever tomorrow
A presence that demands moments of dawdle
Thrumming of the skin begins to throttle
You electrify my very being
A union so calm and ultimately freeing
Never have I met a more perfect person
You are my destiny to which I am certain

Because

We were so young and so naive
Though we believed we'd never leave
We thought we'd be together for all eternity
But things don't always go as planned you see,
because

We said goodbye and went our separate ways
But at night I'd still think of all the days
Together loving, laughing, and being authentic
And all the memories of us made me home sick

Time passed and we both moved on
We were busy with our own lives and gone
But fate had other plans in mind
After necessary time, it was you I'd find

We talked, we laughed, and we reminisced
We both had changed, but that us still exists
And we found that our fire burned brighter
And there was still so much left to desire
Because

With you by my side, my spirit was whole
And I knew that I'd never guess, I would know
It would grow from what it once was
My love for you, because

Because

Truth Within

It buzzes under the skin
A subtle vibration looming beneath
Always prodding, pounding, and pleading to get
out
Swaying of the equilibrium a constant reminder

Do they see it
Does it thrum inside every being
Can it be observed by passing strangers
Is it sensed like a badly kept secret

Not a darkness but a barrier
Forever lingers keeping the truth at bay
If the layer cracks, will it need repaired
Or perhaps a truer interior lies in wait

A familiar essence occupies the mind
A long lost friend you had forgotten
The part of you buried long ago
But a memory of them still remains

Hampered by the experience of juvenility
An old spirit swells with freedom
A soul fragment that was once missing
Now reunites and heals the hollow within

Do You See What I See?

Do you see what I see?
In the moments of candid
When you're soft and free
And you're aura enchanted

Do you see what I see?
When things go unexpected
And your eyes fill with worry
But touch makes you feel protected

Do you see what I see?
When the small things make you smile
And my heart lights up with glee
And I imagine us down the isle

I hope you see what I see
Because I want it for life
Connected to you for eternity
Lucky to be called your wife

Breakthrough

Trudging through the sludge
A resistance that bears it's weight
Slowly forcing you away
A pressure that may combust
How do you combat it?
A strength of will?
Giving in to it's power?
You take a stand
Fire ignites and pulses through you
The heat melts into your surroundings
You permiate through the barrier
Seeing past the smog
Into a new future

Still of the Night

In the still of the night,
As I lay in my bed,
I think of you and how,
I wish you were here with me instead.

I close my eyes and try,
To drift off into sleep,
But all I can think about,
Is the love that runs deep.

I miss your touch and your kiss,
I miss your warmth by my side,
I long for the day,
When we can be together and not hide.

So I lay here and wait,
For the dawn to break and the morning to come,
Hoping that with the new day,
I will be able to hold you and come undone.

Joy

The sun shines bright
On this beautiful day
I am filled with joy
In every single way

The birds sing a song
As they fly through the sky
I am grateful for this life
No need to ask why

So let's take a moment
To stop and appreciate
The beauty that surrounds us
It's never too late

Nature Whispers

The world spins round and round
A never-ending dance
Sometimes lost and sometimes found
But always given a chance

The sky stretches out so wide
A canvas for the sun and moon
The stars glisten on the side
And light the way, a guiding boon

The grass grows tall and green
A carpet for the earth
The flowers bloom and preen
A celebration of their birth

The wind whispers through the trees
A secret song, a gentle breeze
The river flows, a constant ease
A natural rhythm, a soothing peace

Hues of Life

Indigo waves crash down
Mist bringing up on a red dawn
Envy of it's beauty turning green
Sadness of the morning blue
The yellow of the day rises
While the orange heat brings a flame
Blazing the crimson insides of life
Bruised purple with exuberance

Fog

Sadness fills my heart,
Like a heavy autumn fog,
Hiding the sun's light

Kiss me

Kiss me like you're running out of air
As a rememberance of memories shared
Days full of laughter and tears
A fear there aren't enough days or years

Kiss me like it's the first time
Our lips embrace with a feeling sublime
An urge so strong it's hard to contain
But a heavy love will always remain

Kiss me even if we're in darkness
That moment of intimacy a light caress
Keeping the fire inside us lit
A time to look back and be reminiscent

Kiss me as I kiss you
A painting of love that is true
Kiss me as I kiss you
All of the days after we say I do

Safety

You are my home
A place to run to for shelter
When the winds are fierce
And the barrier seems impenetrable
I see your beacon
A guiding force breaking through
Illuminating my journey back
Breathing air into dense lungs
Kissing away the agony
Lulling me into restful arms
My safe place

Memory of you

The memory of you lingers still
A flame that burned so bright and true
I thought that love had had its fill
But now I see it's back for you

The pain has faded with the time
The wounds have healed and left no trace
And in my heart, a love so fine
Has found its way back to this place

I never thought that I'd return
To feelings that I thought were gone
But love can often take a turn
And bring us back where we belong

So now I stand before you, dear
With open heart and open arms
And all I ask, just hold me near
And keep this love that's free from harm

For you and I, we've come so far
And through the years, our love remains
A love that's stronger than a scar
A love that forever sustains

Grounded Darkness

Depression clouds my days with grey
A weight that drags me down each way
A constant ache that won't subside
A pain that leaves me paralyzed

It steals my joy and dims my light
And leaves me with a endless night
No matter what I do or say
It seems to always be this way

It's like a fog that won't lift
And every day is just a gift
A battle that I must fight
In hopes of finding light

But still, I press on and strive
For a brighter day, a chance to survive
And though it's hard, I'll stand my ground
And fight this darkness that surrounds

My Air

You are the light in my darkest days
The beat in my heart, the rhythm of my ways
Your smile is the sun, your touch is the breeze
You make everything better, you bring peace

Your laugh is a song, your eyes are the stars
Together we conquer, together we are
You complete me in ways I never knew
I am grateful for you, my love, my truth

Forever and always, till the end of time
You are the one, you are my rhyme
I love you more every moment we share
You are my everything, my love, my air

Shallow Waters

17

Our love that was yellow had begun to gray
An unknowing decent towards strangers
Harrowing feelings of uncertainty
The accumulation of them always lingered

How could we not have noticed?
Slipping further from each other
Drifting away like fallen wood in a flowing river
The current of life harder to wade through

Could we have swam harder?
Were we one stroke away from reunion?
Or would we have gotten swept under
Unable to resurface to safety

Beauty of a Day

A skyline of trees breathing in unison
Softening the air around us
Rain watering the day for bloom
Washing away the pollen, the dust
The sun in the horizon illuminates the day
A warm glare melting away the unnecessary